HENRI CARTIER-BRESSON

Henri Cartier-Bresson

Introduction by Michael Brenson

PANTHEON BOOKS, NEW YORK.

CENTRE NATIONAL DE LA PHOTOGRAPHIE, PARIS.

On the cover: Salerno, Italy, 1953.

Library of Congress Cataloging in Publication Data

Cartier-Bresson, Henri, 1908-
Henri Cartier-Bresson

Bibliography: p.
1. Photography, Artistic. 2. Cartier-Bresson, Henri, 1908-
I. Title. TR654.C366 1985 779'.092'4 85-42849
ISBN 0-394-74083-1

Manufactured in France / First American Edition
24689753

DIALOGUE BETWEEN
THE EYE AND THE HEART

Whenever I have visited a retrospective of Cartier-Bresson, the range of people in the galleries has mirrored, to some degree, the range of faces and expressions in the photographs on the walls. Not only adults but adolescents and children were eager to know what he has known, to go where he has been. It did not take many images - the wizened Chinamen perhaps, or the carpeted landscapes of India, or the French men and women stuffing their corpulent bodies on the banks of the Seine - to convince them that where he would lead them would be a journey not only through time and space but into themselves.

Cartier-Bresson is one of the few 20th century artists to suggest the degree to which art can still be an expression of a common humanity. He has seen the world, and it is one place. Whether he is photographing hoboes or kings, whether his setting is the Soviet Union, China or the United States, it is one human comedy. We are all people; and people still have to do first of all with pride and envy and laughter and love and indolence and fear.

This book presents a sampling of how much and how well he has seen. There is a political consciousness at work here, and a political position. Because it grows out of a reverence for people and a need not to judge but to share and understand, that position is not and has never been intrusive. It is, however, clear. The book begins with the bristling godfather type in Marseilles and ends with the naked arm and foot of a prisoner thrust defiantly out of a prison cell in the United States. In the middle of the book, a young couple on a train is trying to wrestle some sleep from the Romanian night.

In front of his subjects, in the presence of people, situations and events, Cartier-Bresson's creative effort and energy have been directed outside himself. "Everyone has got some preconceptions," he has said, "but you have to readjust them in front of reality. Reality has the last word." His overriding need has been to "discover" the other, to see and sense the visual configuration in which a person will be revealed, in which a situation or event will allow itself to be seen. To satisfy that need demands an extraordinary discretion. "Approach the subject on tiptoe, even if it is a still-life."

With his kind of concern, with what Hilton Kramer described as his "tremendous appetite for experience," there is something in Cartier-Bresson's work for everyone. For children there is the strength and clarity of his familiar, yet strange images; and there are all the little people, like themselves, in the photographs. Who are those kids seen through the hole blasted through the rubble of Seville? Who is the French kid strutting through the market of the Rue Mouffetard, displaying the bottles of red wine he has been entrusted to bring home as if they were big game trophies? And the little black girl in the white dress, gliding with such dignity by the shack in New Orleans - what is her story?

Perhaps children, with their curiosity, respond to Cartier-Bresson's questions - pick up even better than adults that his work, however decisive and direct it seems, is very much about questions. "Each time you click, it's a question mark. It's a "why" I'm interested in, much more than the answers." That the almost sculptural monumentality of the photographs should often be used in the service of what is open-ended and unknown is one of the many paradoxes that makes the works so complex and explosive. For older people, the interest of the photographs may be human - a way of feeling, of making contact with others - or historical. Cartier-Bresson has been everywhere, has seen almost all the actors and stages of the human comedy. He has seen the earthiness and immobility of the Soviet Union, the frenzy and stillness of Asia, the hopes and ferocity of the United States, the culture and collaboration of France. He has chronicled the coronation of George VI, the funeral of Gandhi, the uprising of May 1968.

While his photographs are a celebration, they are also a point of orientation and a warning. They are a way of measuring the present against the past. "Nothing is more revealing than to compare a country with what it once was, looking for the thread of continuity and for those things which have changed." They are a way of remembering what we are and the little we know, and how easy it is to forget everything.

Then there is the artistic interest of the photographs. Cartier-Bresson's works are so well composed, what Lincoln Kirstein called their "abstract underpinning" is so thoroughly in the service of the main theme, that the best photographs never lose their interest and spark. It is through the composition, which is never posed but always photographed as it is perceived, that the people and situations yield up their meaning and weight. "It is by means of form, by careful plastic organization, that our thoughts and emotions become communicable."

Look at the 1944 photograph of an almost incapacitated Matisse. His self-assurance and prodigious concentration are suggested not only by the way he holds the dove while drawing, but by the way the photograph fixes his body within a dark diagonal axis that contrasts with the light, fluttery quality of the doves and most of the rest of the photograph.

Look at the 1953 photograph of three men, perhaps workers, staring at the ceremonially dressed academician about to enter a taxi in Paris. The more one experiences the relationship between the straight lines, curves and diagonals, the more bitter the image becomes.

Cartier-Bresson's ability to see an event literally taking form - defining itself through a clear and distinct visual configuration - is remarkable in itself. His ability to fix that event at the one and only moment when the pieces fit into a finished puzzle, at the instant when chaos coalesces into order before dissolving into chaos again - and to be able to do this time after time - is hard to imagine. It demands a special balance between attentiveness and detachment, expectancy and patience.

It also involves the rarest kind of union between the photographer and his camera. The camera is as much a part of him as his hand or his head. It is because his visual intelligence and refinement are so embodied, so much a way of sensing and participating in the jagged and insistent rhythms of the world around him, that his work reminds us what using our eyes - really using our eyes - can mean.

There are many examples in this book of Cartier-Bresson's ability to see and capture the meaning of a person or situation. The 1938 "Cardinal Pacelli at Montmartre" consists of a crowd of people milling about a cardinal, who is visiting what was then one of the poorer sections of diamond-like structure.

In front of the cardinal is a woman; to the left is an assistant, to the right, kissing the cardinal's hand, is a young man.

The scene seems familiar and simple, one that takes place every time an important religious official mixes with the populace of a foreign country. The more one looks, however, the more loaded the scene becomes. The cardinal and the devout woman look at each other in a way that suggests her longing for him has moved him. The man kissing the cardinal's hand was clearly hoping, however, that, at least for a moment, he would have the cardinal's undivided attention. He looks almost jilted. The cardinal's assistant looks down at the woman in a patronizing, contemptuous way that suggests that for him, too, the cardinal's attention is a major concern.

What makes the photograph finally so haunting is a peripheral figure. Behind the man kissing the cardinal's hand is a small, darker, pug-nosed woman. She is the kind of humble person that all such occasions are, in principle, about. She is excluded from the scene, however, outside the charmed circle, outside the diagonal axis linking together the cardinal and the policemen, which suggests a complicity between church and state. She has come to be near the cardinal. She is clearly a believer, yet the main scene does not, will not include her. Through her the antiseptic surface of this event - and all events like it - is sanded away. What is left is a fatuous and even cruel piece of religious propaganda.

The photograph is a world. "I am after," Cartier-Bresson has said, "the one unique picture whose composition possesses such vigor and richness, and whose content so radiates outwards from it, that this single picture is a whole story in itself."

Much has been written about the relationship between Cartier-Bresson's photographs and painting and the degree to which his photography comes out of the classical, constructive tradition that includes such French painters as Poussin, Chardin and Cézanne. For some, that pictorial connection is a great strength. For those who believe photography should be an independent medium, with its own references and concerns, the connection with painting is a weakness.

Either way, what is obscured is the degree to which Cartier-Bresson's photography is different from painting. He was trained as a painter, and he makes no bones about his debt to and love for painting. His work raises issues, however, that perhaps only photography can raise now, issues that the mainstream of contemporary art, particularly in America, has long since flushed out to sea. It is really only by defining the ways in which CB's photography is different from painting in general and modernism in particular that the real stature of his work becomes clear.

Cartier-Bresson has said that Surrealism was a formative influence on him. The Surrealists understood and went to great lengths to convince others of the density and magic of everyday life; in this sense, his debt to them is clear. They showed us that nothing, absolutely nothing in our lives is perceived with neutrality. When we really look at the objects around us - a lamp, a table, a chair - they seem to be alive.

With all the attention the Surrealists paid to the object, however, with all the weight they put on everyday things, their real interest was, I think, not the object but the subject. Everything arouses some emotion because in some way it reflects our interior world. It was that world that interested them. What was outside was only really important because it could stir up that world in new ways. The Surrealists spent a lot of time praising the world outside us; they ended up damning it by making it their tool. After them, the modernist focus became, increasingly, the artist and the language he uses.

The gap between Cartier-Bresson and modernism in general could hardly be more absolute. Since his interest really has been people and the integrity of the world outside him, he has never found the modernist and postmodernist play pen of art, language and the self particularly seductive. Because he really has been able to do justice to what he has seen - as it is - his work challenges the subjectivism of contemporary art and defines an altogether different arena.

What if - as his work suggests - brute life is not all that brute? What if there are instants when the seemingly blind movements of time coalesce into an order that is as profound and as revelatory as any created by art? What if that order is objective, outside us, there whether we see it or not? What if it can be captured and presented in a way that does it justice?

Cartier-Bresson's work also questions certain major assumptions underlying the presentday perception of art in general. It is a cliché by now that art can order life. When someone discusses the order in the work of an artist like

Chardin, what is implied is that the artist has created that order. He has imposed an order that is not really there. Art may stop movement, stop time, but time, in fact, stops for no one and nothing. One of the common arguments against classical art is that it is ideal. If the order is not based on anything real, it is always, therefore, to some degree, a consolation and a lie. Maybe time stops for no one, but what if - as Cartier-Bresson's work suggests - the components of a moment somehow, miraculously, come together, forming an order that in terms of that moment makes sense? What if the blind movements of time decide occasionally to get themselves together and wink at us; and allow us, with a camera at the least, to wink back?

If the photographs of Cartier-Bresson can ask these questions, it is because he has been able to establish and maintain a dialogue between the eye and the heart. "Without passion, without working with the emotion of the heart and the enjoyment of the eye, nothing vital can be put down."The ability not just to look at but to see the world outside him - and to use his eyes to enable us to see it with him - challenges yet another major modernist assumption.

Mainstream contemporary art gave up on seeing as a viable way of approaching and rendering reality (the approach of the hyper-realists was too self-conscious and stylized to contradict this). For one thing, the idea of objective vision was pretty much blown up by the end of the 19th century. Some of the Impressionists and Cézanne had tried to be true to what they saw; what they produced was always, however, marked by who they were. If what one sees is inseparable from the person doing the looking, why is an approach based on vision better than any other?

Reinforcing the shift away from trying rigorously to be true to what one sees was modernism's belief that approaching the world through vision meant automatically establishing a relationship of distance and control. Trying to understand or relate to something primarily with one's eyes meant - it was said - remaining apart, treating what one was trying to understand as a thing. Vision as the primary means of orientation was considered, therefore, alienating and hierarchical.

The photographs of Cartier-Bresson suggest, however, that maybe this, too, needs to be rethought. Guided by his eyes, which in turn are guided by his heart, his work comes close to doing full justice to all that he has seen and tried to understand. Far from distancing him from his subjects, his approach establishes an immediate intimacy, an intimacy that becomes - with the snap of the camera - a union.

"Everything is interesting," Cartier-Bresson has said. "Everything is new." For Cézanne and Giacometti, too, to look, really to look, meant constantly seeing the world as if for the first time. Their work has a freshness and a link with the world around them that have become rare. There may come a time when more than a handful of American painters will rediscover the integrity and intelligence of a particular French visual tradition and recognize that with all that American art has gained, something has also been lost.

Michael Brenson

1. Allées du Prado, Marseilles, France, 1932.

2. Quai Saint-Bernard, Paris, 1932.

3. Sienna, Italy, 1933.

4. Quai de Javel, Paris, 1932.

5. Behind the Gare Saint-Lazare, Paris, 1932.

6. Marseilles, France, 1932.

7. Irène and Frédéric Joliot-Curie, Paris, 1945.

8. Valencia, Spain, 1933.

9. Brussels, 1932.

10. Madrid, 1933.

11. Barrio Chino, Barcelona, Spain, 1933.

12. Seville, Spain, 1933.

13. Trieste, Italy, 1933.

14. Roman amphitheater, Valencia, Spain, 1933.

15. Tivoli, Italy, 1933.

16. Cordoba, Spain, 1933.

17. Alicante, Spain, 1932.

18. Seville, Spain, 1932.

19. Castille, Spain, 1953.

20. Henri Matisse, Vence, France, 1944.

21. M., 1967.

22. Palais-Royal, Paris, 1960.

23. Paris, 1952.

24. New York, 1947.

25. Hyde Park, London, 1938.

26. Alberto Giacometti, 1961.

27. Hyères, France, 1932.

28. On the banks of the Marne, France, 1938.

29. Rue Mouffetard, Paris, 1954.

30. Brie, France, June, 1968.

31. Canteen for workers constructing the Hotel Metropole, Moscow, 1954.

32. Rumania, 1975.

33. Irkoutsk, Siberia, U.S.S.R., 1972.

34. Fortress of Peter and Paul, Leningrad, U.S.S.R., 1973.

35. The Hudson and Manhattan, New York, 1946.

36. New England, U.S.A., 1947.

37. Trafalgar Square the day of George VI's coronation, London, 1938.

38. Cardinal Pacelli in Montmartre, Paris, 1938.

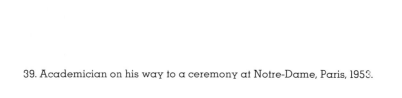
39. Academician on his way to a ceremony at Notre-Dame, Paris, 1953.

40. Sale of gold in the last days of the Kuomintang, Shanghai, China, 1949.

41. Last days of the Kuomintang, Peking, 1949.

42. Anniversary celebration for the Maharaja of Baroda, India, 1947.

43. Games in a refugee camp, Kurukshetra, India, 1948.

44. India, 1947.

45. Srinagar, Kashmir, 1948.

46. Ahmedabad, India, 1965.

47. Athens, 1953.

48. Sifnos, Greece, 1961.

49. Aquila degli Abruzzi, Italy, 1952.

50. Mexico, 1964.

51. Arizona, 1947.

52. Tennessee, U.S.A., 1947.

53. Ireland, 1963.

54. Tralee, Ireland, 1963.

55. Holland, 1953.

56. New Orleans, U.S.A., 1947.

57. Mexico, 1934.

58. Mexico, 1934.

59. Calle Cuauhtemocztin, Mexico, 1934.

60. Volcano of Popocatepetl, Mexico, 1964.

61. Funeral of a Kabuki actor, Japan, 1965.

62. Hungary, 1965.

63. Cell of a model prison, U.S.A., 1975.

BIOGRAPHY

1908. Born on August 22, 1908, at Chanteloup, Seine-et-Marne. Secondary studies at the Lycée Condorcet. No diplomas.

1923. He gets excited about painting and the attitude of the Surrealists.

1927-28. He studies painting with André Lhote.

1931. Adventure trip in the Ivory Coast, where he remains one year. Back in Europe, he makes his first photographs.

1932. His first photographs, exhibited at the Julien Levy Gallery in New York, are then presented by Ignacio Sanchez Mejias and Guillermo de Torre at the Club Atheneo in Madrid. Charles Peignot publishes his first photographs in "Arts et Métiers Graphiques."

1934. He leaves for Mexico where he remains one year with an ethnographic expedition. He exhibits his photographs at the Palacio de Bellas Artes.

1935. He lives in the United States and studies film making with Paul Strand. He makes no photographs.

1936 and 1939. He is second assistant to Jean Renoir for directing, with Jacques Becker and André Zvoboda.

1937. He produces a documentary film on hospitals in Republican Spain: "Victoire de la vie."

1940. Taken prisoner by the Germans, he succeeds in escaping after two unsuccessful attempts.

1943. He takes part in the MNPGD, a clandestine movement of help for prisoners and escaped prisoners.

He produces for the Editions Braun photographic portraits of artists, painters and writers (Matisse, Bonnard, Braque, Claudel...).

1944-45. He joins a group of professionals who photograph the liberation of Paris. He produces "Le Retour," a documentary about the return of war prisoners and of deported people.

1946. He spends more than a year in the United States to complete a "posthumous" exhibition which the Museum of Modern Art of New York had initiated when he was believed dead during the war.

1947. Henri Cartier-Bresson starts with Robert Capa, David Seymour, and George Rodger, the co-operative agency Magnum Photos.

1948-49-50. He spends three years in the Orient, in particular in India, Burma, Pakistan, China (during the last six months of the Kuomintang and the first six of the People's Republic of China), and in Indonesia when it becomes independent.

1952-53. He lives in Europe.

1954. Henri Cartier-Bresson is the first photographer to be admitted into the USSR after restoration of international relations.

1958-59. He returns to China for three months on the occasion of the tenth anniversary of the People's Republic.

1960. From Cuba, where he makes a report, he returns after thirty years to Mexico where he stays for four months. He then goes to live in Canada.

1965. He lives for six months in India and three in Japan.

1966. Henri Cartier-Bresson leaves the Magnum agency which retains, however, the distribution rights of his archives. As before, his photographs are printed by Pictorial Service in Paris.

1969. He prepares an exhibition which will be held at the Grand Palais in 1970: "En France"; and produces in the U.S. two documentaries for C.B.S. News.

Since 1974. He devotes himself to drawing.

1981. "Grand Prix National de la Photographie." Paris, France.

Public Collections (400 photos).
Menil Foundation, Houston, Texas.
Bibliothèque nationale, Paris.
Victoria and Albert Museum, London.
University of Fine Arts, Osaka, Japan.

BIBLIOGRAPHY

**1947. The Photographs
of Henri Cartier-Bresson.**
Monograph published by the Museum
of Modern Art in New York.

1952. Images à la sauvette.
Text and photographs by Henri
Cartier-Bresson. Cover by Matisse.
A work conceived and produced by
Tériade. Editions Verve, Paris.
American edition: "The Decisive
Moment," Simon and Schuster, New York.

1954. Les Danses à Bali.
Text by Antonin Artaud about the
Balinese Theater, and commentaries by
Béryl de Zoete. Delpire Editeur, Paris.

1954. D'une Chine à l'autre.
Preface by Jean-Paul Sartre. Delpire
Editeur, Paris.

1955. Les Européens.
Photographs and introduction by Henri
Cartier-Bresson. Cover by Joan Miró.
A work conceived and produced by
Tériade. Editions Verve, Paris.

**1955. Moscou, vu
par Henri Cartier- Bresson.**
Delpire Editeur, Paris.

1958. Henri Cartier-Bresson. Fotografie.
Text by Anna Farova. Photographs
by Henri Cartier-Bresson, design by
Robert Delpire. Statni nakladatelstvi
krasne literatury hudby a umenu,
narodni podnik, Prague and Bratislava.

**1963. Photographies
de Henri Cartier- Bresson.**
Delpire Editeur, Paris.

1964. China.
Photographs and notes on fifteen
months spent in China. English text
by Barbara Miller, Bantam Books,
New York.

1966. The Galveston that was.
Text by Howard Barstone. Photographs
by Ezra Stoller and Henri Cartier-
Bresson. Macmillan Company, New
York, and the Museum of Fine Arts,
Houston.

1968. L'homme et la machine.
Photographs by Henri Cartier-Bresson,
preceded by an introduction by
Etiemble. A work produced under the
auspices of I.B.M. Editions du Chêne,
Paris.

1968. Flagrants délits.
Delpire Editeur, Paris.

1968. Impression de Turquie.
For the Bureau of Tourism and
Information of Turkey, with an
introduction by Alain Robbe-Grillet.

1970. Vive la France.
Text by François Nourissier.
Photographs by Henri Cartier-Bresson.
Published by the Sélection du
Reader's Digest, Robert Laffont, Paris.

1972. The Face of Asia.
Introduction by Robert Shaplen.
Published by John Weatherhill (New
York and Tokyo), and by Orientations
Ltd. (Hong-Kong). French edition:
"Visage d'Asie," Editions du Chêne,
Paris.

**1973. The Decisive Moment.
Henri Cartier-Bresson.**
Material for audiovisual teaching
(carrousel of photographs and
booklet), published in the collection
"Images of Man," edited by Scholastic
Magazines, Inc., New York.

**1981. Henri Cartier-Bresson:
Photographe.**
Text by Yves Bonnefoy. Delpire
Editeur, Paris. American, British,
German, and Japanese editions.

1983. Ritratti: 1928-1982 (portraits).
I Grandi Fotografi, Fabbri, Milano.

EXHIBITIONS

Photographs.

1932. First exhibition at the Julien Levy Gallery in New York, and at the Cercle Atheneo in Madrid.

1934. Exhibition with Manuel Alvarez Bravo at the Palacio de Bellas Artes, Mexico.

1935. Exhibition with Walker Evans at the Julien Levy Gallery in New York.

1947. "Posthumous" exhibition at the Museum of Modern Art, New York (300 photographs).

1948. Exhibition in Bombay.

1952. Exhibition at the Institute of Contemporary Arts, London.

1953. Exhibition in Florence.

1955. Exhibition of four hundred photographs at the Musée des Arts décoratifs in Paris. This exhibition then circulates in different museums in Europe; in the United States and Canada; in Japan.

1964. Exhibition at the Phillipps Collection, Washington.

1965. Second retrospective first presented in Tokyo, then at the Musée des Arts décoratifs in Paris (1966-1967). The exhibition then goes to New York (1968), London (1969), Amsterdam, and also in Rome, Villa Medicis, Zurich, Leverkusen, Bremen, Milan, Cologne, and Aspen.

1970. Exhibition "En France" at the Grand Palais in Paris. This exhibition will then circulate throughout France until 1976. Then presented in the United States (1970), in the USSR at the Manège in Moscow (1972),

in Yugoslavia (1973), in Australia, and in Japan (1974).

1974. Exhibition about Russia (1953-1974), at the International Center of Photography in New York.

1975. Homage to Henri Cartier-Bresson at the Triennale Internationale de la Photographie, presented by Michel Terrapon, in Fribourg.

1981. In collaboration with the International Center of Photography in New York, Robert Delpire presents an exhibition which will circulate for three years in the principal museums in Europe and in the United States.

1982. Museum of Modern Art, Mexico.

1983. Institut français, Stockholm. Museum of Modern Art, Oxford.

1984. "Paris à vue d'œil," Musée Carnavalet, Paris.

Drawings.

1975. First exhibition at the Carlton Gallery, New York.

1976. Exhibition at the galerie Bischofsberger, in Zurich.

1976. Exhibition at the galerie Lucien Henry, Forcalquier.

1981. Exhibition at the Musée d'Art moderne de la Ville de Paris.

1982. Exhibition at the Modern Art Museum, in Mexico City, and in Monterey.

1983. Pavillon d'Art Contemporain, Milan.

FILMS

Second assistant director to Jean Renoir in 1936 for "La vie est à nous" and "Une partie de campagne," in 1939 for "La Règle du jeu."

Henri Cartier-Bresson produces:
1937. Victoire de la vie.
Documentary about hospitals in Republican Spain; with cameraman Jacques Lemare.

1944-45. Le Retour.
Documentary on the return of war prisoners and deported people, produced by OWI and the Ministère des prisonniers, with Lieutenant Banks, Captain Krimsky, and producer Noma Ratner.

1969-70. Two documentaries for C.B.S. News: "Impressions of California," with cameraman Jean Boffety; and "Southern Exposures," with cameraman Walter Dombrow.

Films using a tracking television camera, with photographs by Henri Cartier-Bresson:

1963-64. Five films of fifteen minutes on Germany, for the Suddeutscher Rundfunk, Munich.

1963. Midlands at play and at work, for ABC Television, New York.

1964. Québec, for the Canadian Film Board.

1967. Flagrants délits, produced by Robert Delpire. Original music by Diego Masson. Delpire production, Paris.

1970. Images de France, film by Liliane de Kermadec for the O.R.T.F. Unité Trois Production.

1975. Why New Jersey, for the National Education Television, New York, Channel 13.

PANTHEON PHOTO LIBRARY

American Photographers of the Depression
Eugène Atget
Henri Cartier-Bresson
Bruce Davidson
Early Color Photography
Robert Frank
André Kertész
Jacques-Henri Lartigue
Duane Michals
Helmut Newton
The Nude
Alexander Rodchenko
W. Eugene Smith
Weegee

The Pantheon Photo Library:
a collection conceived and produced by the
National Center of Photography in Paris
under the direction of Robert Delpire.